Beginner-Friendly Crochet

by Rita Weiss and

Mary Ann Frits

Leisure Arts, Inc.

Maumelle, Arkansas

Produced by

Production Team

Creative Directors:	Jean Leinhauser and Rita Weiss
Pattern Testers:	Carrie Cristiano
	Tammy Layte
Book Design:	Linda Causee

Diagrams © 2015 by The Creative Partners™LLC

Reproduced by special permission

We have made every effort to ensure that these instructions are accurate and complete. We cannot, however, be responsible for human error, typographical mistakes or variations in individual work

Published by Leisure Arts, Inc.

© 2015 by Leisure Arts, Inc.
104 Champs Boulevard, Ste. 100
Maumelle, AR 72113-6738
www.leisurearts.com

ISBN-13: 978-1-4647-3369-7

Introduction

Have you recently learned to crochet? Did someone teach you, or have you taken a class, or perhaps you taught yourself by following a web site online?

Welcome to a wonderful world!

But be aware, however, because here comes the hard part. You are certain that you understand the basics, that you can work with that crochet hook exactly as you were taught, but the patterns you find online or in magazines seem too difficult. There are some easy patterns, but they look like they'll produce the ugliest results.

Here in this book are the answers to your problem.

Here we've collected the kinds of patterns that we used in our early crocheting days. Here you'll find patterns for projects that we enjoyed making and that we enjoyed using or were happy to give as gifts.

But most important of all; all of the patterns are intended for beginners just like you.

So join us for a walk through the pages of this book. Here you'll find a scarf with pockets for your treasures, an afghan that will make you think you are wrapping yourself in mink, a hat celebrating your favorite team colors, a pair of leg warmers plus many more easy-to-do projects.

Although we've geared this book toward beginners, even an advanced crocheter may very well find it hard to resist some of the fantastic items included here.

If you can't remember exactly what you once learned, and you're confused as to what those abbreviations and symbols mean, just check out pages 45 , 46 and 47 where we give you in-depth explanations of how to work the stitches we've used in these patterns.

So choose a pattern, settle down in an easy chair with a crochet hook and some great yarn. Let the wonderful world of crochet open up for you.

You'll be glad you did!

Stay Warm and Stylish All Winter

This very easy-to-crochet hood is extra long so that it offers double wrapping and double warmth to keep you comfortable on the coldest of days.

SKILL LEVEL

Beginner

FINISHED SIZE

Approx 12" x 74" (30.48 cm x 182.88 cm)

MATERIALS

Worsted weight yarn

[100% acrylic, 3.5 ounces, 147 yards (100 grams, 134 meters) per skein]

    5 skeins self-striping yarn

Note: *Photographed model made with Lion Brand® Landscapes® #204 Desert Spring.*

Size J (6 mm) crochet hook (or size required for gauge)

Yarn needle

GAUGE

12 sts = 4" (10.16 cm)

STITCH GUIDE

Ch: Chain

Dc: Double crochet

INSTRUCTIONS

Ch 38.

Row 1: Dc in 4th ch from hook (beginning 3 skipped chs count as first dc), dc in each remaining ch across, ch 3 (counts as first dc on following rows), turn.

Row 2: Dc in each stitch across, ch 3, turn.

Rep Row 2 until piece measures 74". Finish off and weave in ends.

Finishing

Fold piece in half. Starting at fold, and using yarn needle, sew a 1" seam to form the hood.

Note: *For double warmth, wrap the hood over head, around your neck and back again for additional warmth. For casual wear, the front of the hood should be folded back and sewn in place.*

Classic Cowl

Lovely and dramatic, the perfect addition to any outfit.

SKILL LEVEL

Easy

FINISHED SIZE

Approx 10½" x 34" (26.67 cm x 86.36 cm)

MATERIALS

Worsted weight yarn

[100% acrylic, 5 ounces, 236 yards (141 grams, 215 meters) per skein]

    1 skein multi-color

Note: *Photographed model made with Red Heart® Super Saver® #932 Zebra*

Size J (5.5 mm) crochet hook (or size required for gauge)

Yarn needle

GAUGE

(Dc, ch 1) 8 times = 4"

STITCH GUIDE

Ch: Chain

Dc: Double crochet

Hdc: Half double crochet

Sp: Space

INSTRUCTIONS

Ch 37.

Row 1 (right side): Hdc in 3rd ch from hook (beg 2 skipped chs count as first hdc), * ch 1, skip next ch, hdc in next ch; repeat from * 16 times more, ch 2 (counts as first hdc on following rows), turn.

Row 2: * Hdc in next ch-1 sp, ch 1; rep from * 16 times more; skip next hdc, hdc in 2nd ch of beg 2 skipped chs, ch 2, turn.

Row 3: * Hdc in next ch-1 sp, ch 1; rep from * 16 times more; skip next hdc, hdc in 2nd ch of turning ch-2, ch 2, turn.

Rep Row 3 until piece measures 34" from beg. Finish off and weave in ends.

Finishing

Hold piece with right side of short ends together. With yarn needle and working through both thicknesses, sew short ends together. Turn right side out.

Delightful Dishcloth

Add some spice to the boring job of washing dishes when you add this easy-to-make crocheted dishcloth.

SKILL LEVEL

Easy ◼◼◻◻

FINISHED SIZE

Approx 8" (20.32 cm) in diameter

MATERIALS

Worsted weight cotton yarn (4)

[100% combed cotton, 2 ounces, 98 yards
(56.7 grams, 89.6 meters) per ball]

   1 ball variegated

Note: *Photographed model made with Red Heart®
Crème de la Crème #945 Orangetones*

Size H (5 mm) crochet hook (or size required for
gauge)

Yarn needle

GAUGE

Round 1 = 1" (2.54 cm) in diameter

STITCH GUIDE

Ch: Chain
Sl st: Slip stitch
Dc: Double crochet

INSTRUCTIONS

Ch 6, join with sl st in first ch to form a ring.

Round 1 (right side): Ch 3 (counts as first dc), 7 dc in
ring: 8 dc. Do not join; mark beginning of rounds.

Round 2: 2 dc in each dc: 16 dc.

Round 3: *2 dc in next dc, dc in next dc, repeat from
* around: 24 dc.

Round 4: *2 dc in next dc, dc in next 2 dc, repeat
from * around: 32 dc.

Round 5: *2 dc in next dc, dc in next 3 dc, repeat
from * around: 40 dc.

Round 6: *2 dc in next dc, dc in next 4 dc, repeat
from * around: 48 dc.

Round 7: *2 dc in next dc, dc in next 5 dc, repeat
from * around: 56 dc.

Round 8: 2 dc in each dc; join with sl st in first dc:
112 dc.

Finish off and weave in ends.

Pocket Scarf

Enjoy this scarf with deep pockets designed to keep your hands warm and your treasures safe.

SKILL LEVEL

Easy

FINISHED SIZE

Approx 10½" x 71" (26.67 cm x 180.34 cm)

MATERIALS

Bulky weight yarn

[100% acrylic, 3 ounces, 135 yards (85 grams, 338 meters) per skein]

    3 skeins white (A)

    3 skeins black (B)

Note: *Photographed model made with Lion Brand® Jiffy® #100 White (A) and #153 Black (B)*

Size J (6 mm) crochet hook (or size required for gauge)

Yarn needle

GAUGE

10 dc = 4" (10.16 cm)

STITCH GUIDE

Ch: Chain

Dc: Double crochet

INSTRUCTIONS

Strip A

With A, ch 16.

Row 1 (wrong side): Dc in 4th ch from hook (beginning 3 skipped chs count as first dc), dc in each rem ch, ch 3 (counts as first dc on following rows), turn.

Row 2 (right side): Dc in each stitch across, ch 3, turn.

Rows 3 through 7: Repeat Row 2.

Row 8: Dc in each stitch across, change to B, ch 3, turn.

Rows 9 through 15: Repeat Row 2.

Row 16: Dc in each stitch across, change to A, ch 3, turn.

Rows 17 through 23: Repeat Row 2.

Row 24: Dc in each stitch across, change to B, ch 3, turn.

Rows 25 through 104: Repeat Rows 9 through 24 five times. At end of last row, do not change color. Finish off.

Strip B

With B, ch 16.

Row 1 (wrong side): Dc in 4th chain from hook (beg 3 skipped chs count as first dc), dc in each remaining ch, ch 3 (counts as first dc on following rows), turn.

Row 2: Dc in each st across, ch 3, turn.

Rows 3 through 7: Repeat Row 2.

Row 8: Dc in each st across, change to A, ch 3, turn.

Rows 9 through 15: Repeat Row 2.

Row 16: Dc in each stitch across, change to B, ch 3, turn.

Rows 17 through 23: Repeat Row 2.

Row 24: Dc in each st across, change to A, ch 3, turn.

Rows 25 through 104: Repeat Rows 9 through 24 five times. At end of last row, do not change color. Finish off.

White Pocket

With A, ch 30.

Row 1: Dc in 4th chain from hook (beg 3 skipped chs count as first dc), dc in each remaining ch, ch 3 (counts as first dc on following rows), turn.

Row 2: Dc in each stitch across, ch 3, turn.

Rows 3 through 12: Repeat Row 2. Finish off.

Black Pocket

With B, work same as White Pocket.

Finishing

With wrong sides together, sew strips together side by side through stitches at the end of each row. Sew one Pocket to each end of scarf. Weave in all ends.

Make Mine Mink

Always wanted to wrap yourself in fur? Here's a chance to wrap yourself in this chenille throw that has much of the same look as expensive fur. And not an animal is harmed.

SKILL LEVEL

Beginner

FINISHED SIZE

Approx 45" x 56" (114.3 cm x 142.24 cm)

MATERIALS

Bulky weight yarn 5

[75% acrylic/18% polyester/7% nylon, 2.5 ounces, 100 yards (71 grams, 91 meters) per skein]

13 skeins brown

Note: *Photographed model made with Lion Brand® Chenille® #126 Brownstone.*

Size N (9mm) crochet hook, or size required for gauge

Yarn needle

GAUGE

10 dc = 5" (12.7 cm)

STITCH GAUGE

Ch: Chain

Dc: Double crochet

INSTRUCTIONS

Loosely ch 90.

Row 1: Dc in 4th ch from hook (beginning 3 skipped chs count as first dc) and in each remaining ch: 88 dc; ch 3 (counts as first dc on following rows) turn.

Row 2: Dc in each dc; ch 3, turn.

Rep Row 2 until piece measures about 56" from beg ch.

Finish off and weave in ends.

Wonderful Ear Warmer

Designed by Laura Bain for Red Heart®

This easy-to-crochet headband is just what you will want to face those cold winter days.

SKILL LEVEL

Easy ◼◼☐☐▭

FINISHED SIZE

Approx 4" x 22" (10.16 cm x 55.88 cm)
in circumference

MATERIALS

Bulky weight yarn

[85% acrylic, 15% polyester, 3.5 ounces, 88 yards
(100 grams, 80 meters) per skein]

    1 skein blue

    1 skein purple

Note: *Photographed model made with Red Heart®
Reflective® #8884 Peacock and #8532 Purple*

Size I (5.5 mm) crochet hook, or size required for
gauge

Yarn needle

GAUGE

10 dc in pattern = 4" (10.16 cm)

STITCH GUIDE

Ch: Chain
Dc: Double crochet

INSTRUCTIONS

With one strand of blue and one strand of purple
held together, ch 12.

Row 1 (right side): Dc in 4th ch from hook
(beginning 3 skipped chs count as first dc), dc in
each rem ch across: 10 dc; ch 3 (counts as first dc
on following rows), turn.

Row 2: Dc in each dc across, ch 3, turn.

Rows 3 through 25: Repeat Row 2.

Row 26: Dc in each dc across, ch 1, turn.

Row 27: Fold piece in half with beginning ch
behind Row 26, working through both thicknesses,
sc in each dc across.

Finish off and weave in ends.

Sunny Coaster

An afternoon cup of tea is certain to taste better when it is served in a cup sitting on a sunny coaster, a perfect project for a beginner crocheter.

SKILL LEVEL

Beginner ⬛⬜⬜⬜

FINISHED SIZE

Approx 4½" x 4½" (11.43 cm x 11.43 cm)

MATERIALS

Worsted weight cotton yarn 🔵4🔵

[100% combed cotton, 2½ ounces, 125 yards (70.9 grams, 114.3 meters) per ball]

    1 ball yellow

Note: *Photographed model made with Red Heart® Crème de la Crème #200 Sunshine*

Size H (5 mm) crochet hook (or size required for gauge)

Yarn needle

GAUGE

12 stitches = 4" (10.16 cm) in pattern

STITCH GUIDE

Ch: Chain

Sc: Single crochet

Dc: Double crochet

INSTRUCTIONS

Ch 18.

Row 1 (right side): Sc in 2nd ch from hook, sc in each remaining ch across: 17 sc; ch 1, turn.

Row 2: Sc in first 2 stitches, * dc in next stitch, sc in next stitch, repeat from * across to last stitch, sc in last stitch, ch 1, turn.

Row 3: Sc in first stitch, * dc in next stitch, sc in next stitch, repeat from * across, turn.

Rows 4 through 15: Repeat Rows 2 and 3 six times.

Finish off and weave in ends.

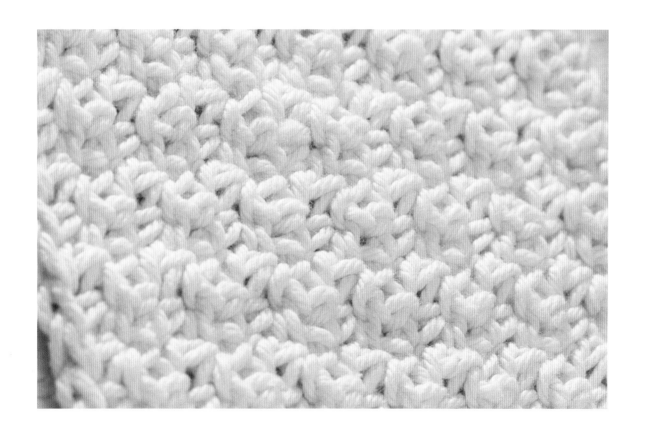

17

Supporting My Team

Designed by Nancy Smith for Red Heart®

With this self-striping yarn, it's easy to show your support for your team. Great for both guys and gals, the scarf will make a great gift.

SKILL LEVEL

Easy

FINISHED SIZE

Approx 10" x 69" (25.40 cm x 175.26 cm) without fringe

MATERIALS

Worsted weight yarn

[100% acrylic, 5 ounces, 244 yards (141 grams, 223 meters) per skein]

3 skeins multi-color

Note: *Photographed model made with Red Heart® Team Spirit™ #984 Red/Grey*

Size K (6.5 mm) crochet hook, or size required for gauge

Yarn needle

GAUGE

13 sts = 4" (10.16 cm)

STITCH GUIDE

Ch: Chain

Sc: Single crochet

Sl st: Slip stitch

Sp: Space

NOTE

Scarf is worked with one yarn. Color changes should occur at the end of row after 6 rows have been worked. But if you are off a bit, your scarf will still look fine.

INSTRUCTIONS

With first color, ch 34.

Row 1: Sc in 2nd ch from hook, *skip next ch, ch 1, sc in next ch; repeat from * across to last ch, sc in last ch: 17 sc and 15 ch-1 sps. Finish off first color. Cut yarn to remove current section of first color.

Row 2: Leaving 4" (10.16 cm) end, join 2nd color with sl st in first sc, ch 1, sc in same sc, *skip next sc, ch 1, sc in next ch-1 sp; repeat from * across to last st, sc in last st, ch 1, turn.

Row 3: Sc in first sc, *skip next sc, ch 1, sc in next ch-1 sp; repeat from * across to last sc, sc in last sc, ch 1, turn.

Rows 4 through 6: Repeat Row 3. Finish off second color.

Repeat Rows 2 through 6 alternating colors for 35 stripes, ending with a stripe of second color.

Last Row: Repeat Row 2 with first color. Do not finish off.

Edging

Turn scarf to work across long side, ch 1, sc in end of each row across, ch 1, sl st in first ch of beginning ch. Finish off.

Repeat on second long side.

Finish off and weave in ends.

Fringe

Use both colors to make fringe. Cut 80 strands of first color and 90 strands of second color, each 10" (25.5 cm) long.

Beginning with second color, attach fringe as follows in first corner stitch: hold 5 strands together and fold in half. With Wrong Side facing, insert hook through first corner stitch on short edge of scarf and draw folded ends of strands through to form loop. Thread ends of strands through loop and pull ends to tighten. Continue attaching fringe in each ch-1 space and in opposite corner stitch across, alternating 2 sections of second color and 2 sections of first color, ending with second color.

Trim strands to even all fringe.

Springtime Scarf

The perfect addition to anyone's springtime wardrobe is this elegant scarf created from a yarn of many colors.

SKILL LEVEL

Easy

FINISHED SIZE

Approx 6" x 60" (15.24 cm x 152.40 cm)

MATERIALS

Light worsted weight yarn

[80% acrylic and 20% nylon, 3 ounces, 290 yards (85 grams, 265 meters) per skein]

    1 skein multi-color

Note: *Photographed model made with Red Heart® Anne Geddes Baby™ #930 Sailboat*

Size I (5.5 mm) crochet hook (or size required for gauge)

Tapestry needle

GAUGE

4 sc = 1"

STITCH GUIDE

Ch: Chain

Sc: Single crochet

Dc: Double crochet

Sl st: Slip stitch

INSTRUCTIONS

Ch 24.

Row 1: Sc in 2nd ch from hook and in each remaining ch across, ch 4 (counts as first double crochet and ch-1 sp on following rows), turn.

Row 2: Skip first 2 sc, (dc in next sc, ch 1, skip next sc) 10 times, ch 4, turn.

Row 3: (Dc in next dc, ch 1) 10 times, dc in 3rd ch of turning ch-3, ch 4, turn.

Row 4: (Dc in next dc, ch 1) 10 times, dc in 3rd ch of turning ch-3, ch 1, turn.

Row 5: Sc in each dc and in each ch-1 sp across to turning ch-4, sc in space formed by turning ch-4, sc in 3rd ch of same turning ch, ch 4, turn.

Repeat Rows 2 through 5 until piece measures 60" from beginning. At end of last row, do not ch 4 or turn.

Edging

Ch 1, working in ends across next long side, work 2 sc in each dc row and sc in each sc row across, ch 1, working in unused lps on opposite side of beginning ch, sc in each ch across, ch 1, working in ends of rows across next long side, work 2 sc in each dc row and sc in each sc row across to last row, ch 1, sc in each sc across last row; join with sl st in beginning ch-1.

Finish off and weave in ends.

Tablet Cozy

Designed by Becky Barker for Red Heart®

Protect your precious electronic tablet by crocheting this easy and attractive cover.

SKILL LEVEL

Easy

FINISHED SIZE

10½" x 7" (26.67 cm x 28.78 cm)

MATERIALS

Worsted weight yarn

[100% acrylic, 7 ounces, 364 yards (198 grams, 333 meters) per skein]

    1 skein blue

Note: *Photographed model made with Red Heart® Super Saver® #3945 Blue Suede*

Size G (4 mm) crochet hook (or size required for gauge)

Yarn needle

GAUGE

14 sts = 4"

STITCH GUIDE

Ch: Chain

Sc: Single crochet

Sl st: Slip stitch

INSTRUCTIONS

Ch 26.

Round 1: Sc in 2nd ch from hook and in next 23 chs, 3 sc in last ch, working on opposite side of beginning ch, sc in next 23 chs, 2 sc in last ch: 52 sc. Do not join; mark beginning of rounds.

Round 2: Sc in each sc around.

Rounds 3 through 33: Repeat Round 2.

Round 34: Sc in each sc around; join with sl st in next sc. Do not finish off.

Ribbing

Row 1: Ch 8, sc in 2nd ch from hook and in next 7 chs, sl st in next 2 sc of Rnd 34, ch 1, turn.

Row 2: Sc in back loop of next 8 sc, ch 1, turn.

Row 3: Sc in back loop of next 8 sc, sl st in next 2 sc on Rnd 34, ch 1, turn.

Rows 4 through 51: Rep Rows 2 and 3 twenty-four times.

Row 52: Working in back loops of last row and unused loops of Row 1, sc in each sc across; sl st in top of Row 1.

Finish off and weave in ends.

Mini Tote

Carry all of your precious possessions in this easy-to-crochet tote.

SKILL LEVEL

Easy

FINISHED SIZE

Approx 8" x 10" (20.32 cm x 25.40 cm) without strap

MATERIALS

Worsted weight yarn

[100% acrylic, 5 ounces, 266 yards (141 grams, 243 meters) per skein]

    3 skeins blue tweed

Note: *Photographed model made with Red Heart® Super Tweed® #7803 Blue Bayou*

Size J (5.5mm) crochet hook, or size required for gauge

Yarn needle

⅞" (2.22 cm) brown button

GAUGE

6 sc = 2" (5.08 cm)

STITCH GUIDE

Ch: Chain

Hdc: Half double crochet

Sp: Space

INSTRUCTIONS

Front/Back (make 2)

Ch 25.

Row 1: Hdc in 3rd ch from hook (beginning 2 skipped chs count as first hdc), hdc in each remaining ch across: 24 hdc; ch 2 (counts as first hdc on following rows), turn.

Row 2: Hdc in each hdc across, ch 2, turn.

Repeat Row 2 until piece measures approx 10" (25.40 cm) from beginning.

Finish off and weave in ends.

Strap

Ch 5.

Row 1: Hdc in first ch (beginning 4 skipped chs count as first hdc and ch-1), ch 3 (counts as first hdc and ch-1 sp on following rows), turn.

Row 2: Hdc in 3rd ch of beginning 4 skipped chs, ch 3, turn.

Row 3: Hdc in 2nd ch of turning ch-3, ch 3, turn.

Repeat Row 3 until piece measures 40" (101.6 cm) from beginning. At end of last row, do not ch 3; do not turn.

Finish off and weave in ends.

Button Flap

Ch 4.

Row 1: Sc in 2nd ch from hook and in each remaining ch across, ch 3 (counts as first hdc and ch-1 sp on following rows), turn.

Row 2: Skip first 2 sc, hdc in next hdc, ch 3, turn.

Row 3: Hdc in 2nd ch of turning ch-3, ch 3, turn.

Rep Row 3 until piece measures 4" (10.16 cm) from beginning. At end of last row, ch 1, turn.

Last Row: Sc in first hdc, sc in next 2 chs of turning ch-3.

Finish off and weave in ends.

Finishing

Sew sides and bottom edges together. Sew ends of strap to inside of top over side seams. Sew one end of button flap to center of back. Sew button to center of front. Buttonhole is formed by ch-1 space on flap.

Leg Warmers

Wear these easy-to-crochet and colorful leg warmers for their warmth or just for the fun.

SKILL LEVEL

Easy

FINISHED SIZE

Approx 8" x 24" long (20.32 cm x 60.96 cm)

MATERIALS

Worsted weight yarn

[100% acrylic, 5 ounces, 236 yards (141 grams, 215 meters) per skein]

    1 skein multi-color (A)

[100% acrylic, 7 ounces, 364 yards (198 grams, 333 meters) per skein]

    1 skein blue (B)

    1 skein pink (C)

    1 skein orange (D)

Note: *Photographed model made with Red Heart® Super Saver® #3939 Blacklight (A), #512 Turqua (B), #722 Pretty 'N' Pink (C) and #254 Pumpkin (D)*

Sizes E (3.5 mm), H (5 mm), K (6.5 mm) crochet hooks (or sizes required for gauges)

Yarn needle

GAUGES

With size E hook, 18 sts = 4" (10.16 cm)

With size G hook, 16 sts = 4" (10.16 cm)

With size K hook, 12 sts = 4" (10.16 cm)

STITCH GUIDE

Ch: Chain

Sc: Single crochet

Sl st: Slip stitch

INSTRUCTIONS

(make 2)

Bottom Ribbing

With E hook and A, ch 16.

Row 1: Sc in 2nd ch from hook and in each remaining ch across: 15 sc; ch 1, turn.

Row 2: Sc in back loop of each stitch across, ch 1, turn.

Rows 3 through 40: Repeat Row 2. At end of Row 40, do not turn. Change to B.

Body

Row 1: Ch 1, working in ends of rows across long side, sc in each row across, turn.

Row 2: Ch 1, sc in each st across: 40 sc; ch 1, turn.

Rep Row 2 until piece measures 6" (15.24 cm) from beginning.

Change to G hook and D.

Repeat Row 2 until piece measures 9" (22.86 cm) from beginning. Change to C.

Repeat Row 2 until piece measures 11" (27.95 cm) from beginning. Change to A.

Repeat Row 2 until piece measures 12" (30.48 cm) from beginning. Change to B.

Repeat Row 2 until piece measures 15" (38.10 cm) from beginning. Change to K hook and D.

Repeat Row 2 until piece measures 18" (45.72 cm) from beginning. Change to B.

Repeat Row 2 until piece measures 21" (53.34 cm) from beginning. At end of last row, ch 18, turn. Change to C.

Top Ribbing

Row 1: Sc in 2nd ch from hook and in each remaining ch across, sl st in next 3 sc on last row of Body, ch 1, turn.

Row 2: Sc in back loop of each stitch across, ch 1, turn.

Row 3: Sc in back loop of each stitch across, sl st in next 4 stitches on last row of Body, ch 1, turn.

Rows 4 through 19: Repeat Rows 2 and 3 eight times.

Row 20: Repeat Row 2.

Row 21: Sc in back loop of each stitch across, sl st in same stitch on Body as last sl st made.

Finish off and weave in ends.

Finishing

Sew side seams.

27

Women's Mittens

Designed by Nancy Anderson for Red Heart®

These simple mittens, which are designed without a definite left or right hand, have an extra long cuff for extra warmth or can be folded at the wrist.

SKILL LEVEL

Easy

FINISHED SIZE

Approx 11½" long x 7½" in circumference
(29.21 cm x 19.05 cm)

MATERIALS

Worsted weight yarn

[100% acrylic, 7 ounces, 364 yards (198 grams, 333 meters) per skein]

    1 skein green (A)

    1 skein dark blue (B)

Note: *Photographed model made with Red Heart® Super Saver® #624 Tea Leaf (A) and #387 Soft Navy (B)*

Size I (5.5 mm) crochet hook (or size required for gauge)

Yarn needle

GAUGE

16 sts = 4" (10.16 cm)

STITCH GUIDE

Ch: Chain

Sc: Single crochet

Sl st: Slip stitch

Decrease: Decrease by drawing up a loop in each of 2 stitches, YO and draw through all 3 loops on hook.

INSTRUCTIONS

(make 2)

Cuff

With B, ch 21.

Row 1: Sc in back loop of 2nd ch from hook and in back loop of each remaining ch across, ch 1, turn: 20 sc.

Row 2: Sc in back loop of each sc across, ch 1, turn.

Rows 3 through 22: Repeat Row 2.

Row 23: Fold piece in half, matching sts of Row 22 with chs of beg ch, working through both thicknesses, sl st in each st across. Do not finish off.

Turn piece inside out.

Hand

Round 1: Ch 1, working in ends of rows across long edge, sl st in each row around; join with sl st in first sl st.

Note: *Mark first st of following rnds.*

Round 2: Ch 1, sc in first 10 stitches, 2 stitches in next stitch, sc in next 10 stitches, 2 sc in next stitch; join with sl st in first sc: 24 sts.

Round 3: Ch 1, sc in first 11 stitches, 2 stitches in next st, sc in next 11 stitches, 2 sc in next st; join with sl st in first sc. 26 st. Change to A.

Round 4: Ch 1, sc in first 12 stitches, 2 stitches in next stitch, sc in next 12 stitches, 2 sc in next stitch; join with sl st in first sc: 28 sts. Change to B.

Round 5: Ch 1, sc in first 13 stitches, 2 stitches in next stitch, sc in next 13 stitches, 2 sc in next stitch; join with sl st in first sc: 30 sts. Change to A.

Round 6: Ch 1, sc in each sc around; join with sl st in first sc. Change to B.

Round 7: Rep Round 6, changing to A at end of rnd.

Rnd 8: Rep Rnd 6.

Round 9: Ch 1, sc in first 26 stitches, ch 5 (thumb hole), skip remaining stitches; join with sl st in first sc: 26 sc, 5 chs. Change to A.

Round 10: Ch 1, sc in each stitch around, join with sl st in first sc: 31 sts. Change to B.

Round 11: Ch 1, sc in each sc around; join with sl st in first sc. Change to A.

Rounds 12 through 19: Repeat Rounds 10 and 11 four times.

Round 20: Ch 1, decrease in first 2 sc, sc in each remaining sc around: 30 sc. Change to B. Do not join; mark beginning of rounds.

Round 21: (Sc in next 13 sts, decrease in next 2 sts) twice: 28 sts. Change to A.

Round 22: (Sc in next 12 stitches, decrease in next 2 sts) twice: 26 sts. Change to B.

Round 23: (Sc in next 11 stitches, decrease in next 2 stitches) twice: 24 sts. Change to A.

Round 24: (Sc in next 10 sts, decrease in next 2 sts) twice: 22 sts. Change to B.

Round 25: Sc in each sc around. Change to A.

Round 26: (Sc in next 9 sts, dec in next 2 sts) twice: 20 sts. Change to B.

Round 27: (Decrease in next 2 sts) 10 times: 10 sts. Change to A.

Round 28: (Decrease in next 2 sts) 10 times: 5 sts. Finish off.

Thumb

Round 1: Join A in first stitch closest to hand, ch 1, sc in each stitch around, join with sl st in first sc: 9 sts. Change to B.

Round 2: Sc in each st around. Change to A.

Round 3: Sc in each st around. Change to B.

Rounds 4 through 7: Repeat Rnds 2 and 3 twice.

Round 8: Decrease in next 2 stitches, sc in next 5 stitches, decrease in next 2 sts: 7 sts.

Change to A.

Round 9: (Decrease in next 2 stitches) 3 times, sc in next sc: 4 sts.

Finish off and weave in ends.

Tween Style Wrister

Designed by Salena Baca for Red Heart®

Keep your hands warm while your fingers do fun things, like crocheting. Quick to do; so make them for your friends in your school colors and cheer your team at the next game.

SKILL LEVEL

Easy

FINISHED SIZE

Approx 6½" long x 7½" in circumference
(16.51 cm x 19.05 cm)

MATERIALS

Worsted weight yarn

[100% acrylic, 7 ounces, 364 yards (198 grams,
333 meters) per skein]

    1 skein orchid (A)

    1 skein purple (B)

Note: *Photographed model made with Red Heart®
Super Saver® #530 Orchid (A) and #358 Lavender (B)*

Size I (5.5 mm) crochet hook (or size required for
gauge)

Yarn needle

GAUGE

13 sts = 4" (10.16 cm)

STITCH GUIDE

Ch: Chain

Sc: Single crochet

Hdc: Half double crochet

Sl st: Slip stitch

INSTRUCTIONS

(make 2)

Cuff

With A, ch 9.

Row 1: Sc in 2nd ch from hook and in each
remaining ch across: 8 sc; ch 1, turn.

Row 2: Sc in back loop of each sc across, ch 1, turn.

Rows 3 through 24: Repeat Row 2.

Row 25: Fold piece in half with beginning ch behind
Row 24, working through both thicknesses, sl st in
each stitch across. Do not finish off.

Turn piece inside out.

Body

Round 1: Ch 1, working in ends of rows across long
edge, hdc in each row around; join with sl st in first
hdc: 24 hdc.

Note: *Mark first st of following rounds.*

Round 2: Ch 1, hdc in each hdc around; join with
sl st in first hdc. Finish off A; join B.

Round 3: Ch 1, sc in each st around; join with
sl st in first sc. Finish off B; join A.

Round 4: Ch 1, hdc in each st around; join with sl st
in first hdc.

Round 5: Repeat Round 4. Finish off A; join B.

Round 6: Repeat Round 3.

Round 7: Ch 1, * hdc in next 7 sc, 2 hdc in next
sc; repeat from * around; join with sl st in first hdc:
27 hdc.

Round 8: Ch 1, hdc in first stitch, skip next 6
stitches (for thumb hole), hdc in next 20 sts; join
with sl st in first hdc: 21 hdc. Finish off A; join B.

Round 9: Repeat Round 3.

Rounds 10 and 11: Repeat Round 4. Finish off A; join B.

Round 12: Repeat Round 3. Finish off B; do not join A.

Weave in ends.

Party Cup Cozy

Make certain that each of your guests has a cozy to keep cold drinks cool, and hot drinks warm.

SKILL LEVEL

Easy ▩▩▢▢

FINISHED SIZE

Approx 2½" high x 7" in circumference (54.61 cm x 17.78 cm)

MATERIALS

Worsted weight cotton yarn 4

[100% Combed cotton, 2 ounces, 98 yards (56.7 grams, 89.6 meters) per ball]

   1 ball multi-color

Note: *Photographed model made with Red Heart® Crème de la Crème #932 Popsicle Bright*

Size H (5 mm) crochet hook (or size required for gauge)

Yarn needle

GAUGE

10 sts = 2" (5.08 cm)

STITCH GUIDE

Ch: Chain

Hdc: Half double crochet

Sc: Single crochet

INSTRUCTIONS

Ch 13.

Row 1 (right side): Hdc in 3rd ch from hook (beginning 2 skipped chs count as first hdc), hdc in each remaining ch across: 12 hdc, ch 2 (counts as first hdc on following rows), turn.

Row 2: Working in back loops, hdc in each stitch across, ch 2, turn.

Rows 3 through 17: Repeat Row 2.

Row 18: Fold piece in half with beginning ch behind Row 17; matching hdc of Row 17 with chs of beginning ch and working through both thicknesses, sc in each hdc across.

Finish off and weave in ends.

Sassy But Sweet Hat and Scarf

What tween wouldn't love wearing this sassy hat and matching scarf!

SKILL LEVEL

Easy

FINISHED SIZE

Scarf: Approx 10" x 70" (25.40 cm x 177.80 cm)

Hat: Fits 22" (55.88 cm) head circumference

MATERIALS

Worsted weight yarn

[100% acrylic, 7 ounces, 370 yards (198 grams, 338 meters) per skein]

> 2 skeins green (A)
>
> 2 skeins white (B)

Note: *Photographed model made with Red Heart® With Love® #1562 Jadeite (A) and #1001 White (B).*

Size J (6 mm) crochet hook (or size required for gauge)

Yarn needle

GAUGE

12 sts = 4" (10.16 cm)

STITCH GUIDE

Ch: Chain

Hdc: Half double crochet

INSTRUCTIONS

Scarf

With A, ch 31.

Row 1 (right side): Hdc in 3rd ch from hook (beginning 2 skipped chs count as first hdc) and in each remaining ch across: 30 hdc; ch 2 (counts as first hdc on following rows), turn.

Row 2: Ch 2, hdc in each stitch across, change to B, ch 2, turn.

Row 3: Ch 2, hdc in each stitch across, ch 2, turn.

Row 4: Ch 2, hdc in each stitch across, change to A, ch 2, turn.

Row 5: Ch 2, hdc in each stitch across, ch 2, turn.

Row 6: Ch 2, hdc in each stitch across, change to B, ch 2, turn.

Repeat Rows 3 through 6 until scarf measures 70" (177.80 cm). At end of last row, do not change color. Finish off and weave in ends.

Hat

With A, ch 31.

Row 1 (right side): Hdc in 3rd ch from hook (beginning 2 skipped chs count as first hdc) and in each remaining ch across: 30 hdc; ch 2 (counts as first hdc on following rows), turn.

Row 2: Ch 2, hdc in each stitch across, change to B, ch 2, turn.

Row 3: Ch 2, hdc in each stitch across, ch 2, turn.

Row 4: Ch 2, hdc in each stitch across, change to A, ch 2, turn.

Row 5: Ch 2, hdc in each stitch across, ch 2, turn.

Row 6: Ch 2, hdc in each stitch across, change to B, ch 2, turn.

Rows 7-18: Repeat Rows 3 through 6 three times.

Rows 19 and 20: Repeat Rows 3 and 4.

Rows 21 through 23: Repeat Row 5.

Row 24: Repeat Row 6.

Rows 25 through 44: Repeat Rows 3 through 6 five times.

At end of last row, do not change color. Finish off and weave in ends.

Finishing

Fold hat at the middle of the wide green stripe with right sides together. Carefully matching stripes, sew side seams, starting at the bottom and continuing to the top. Turn hat right side out and flip up brim.

Got Team Spirit Hat

Designed by Edie Eckman for Red Heart®

**Show your team spirit by making hats in your favorite team colors for all your friends.
This yarn comes in favorite team colors.**

SKILL LEVEL

Easy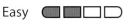

FINISHED SIZE

21" (53.34 cm) circumference

MATERIALS

Worsted weight yarn

[100% acrylic, 5 ounces, 244 yards (141 grams, 223 meters) per skein]

    1 skein multi-color

Note: *Photographed model made with Red Heart® Team Spirit™ #948 Green/Gold or #972 Orange/Black*

Size I (5.5 mm) crochet hook (or size required for gauge)

Yarn needle

GAUGE

11 dc = 4" (10.16 cm)

STITCH GUIDE

Ch: Chain

Sl st: Slip stitch

Dc: Double crochet

INSTRUCTIONS

Ch 4; join with sl st to form a ring.

Round 1: Ch 3 (counts as first dc here and on following rounds), 11 dc in ring, join with sl st in 3rd ch of beginning ch-3: 12 dc.

Round 2: Ch 3, dc in same ch as joining, 2 dc in each remaining dc around, join with sl st in 3rd ch of beginning ch-3: 24 dc.

Round 3: Ch 3, 2 dc in next dc, *dc in next dc, 2 dc in next dc; repeat from * around, join with sl st in 3rd ch of beginning ch-3: 36 dc.

Round 4: Ch 3, dc in next dc, 2 dc in next dc, *dc in next 2 dc, 2 dc in next dc; repeat from * around, join with sl st in 3rd ch of beginning ch-3: 48 dc.

Round 5: Ch 3, dc in next 4 dc, 2 dc in next dc, *dc in next 5 dc, 2 dc in next dc; repeat from * around, join with sl st in 3rd ch of beginning ch-3: 56 dc.

Round 6: Ch 3, dc in each dc around; join with sl st in 3rd ch of beginning ch-3.

Rounds 7 through 14: Repeat Round 6.

Finish off and weave in ends.

Quick and Cozy Afghan

Practice your basic crochet while you create an afghan that will be a warm addition to your home for years.

SKILL LEVEL

Beginner

FINISHED SIZE

Approx 44" x 58" (111.76 cm x 147.32 cm)

MATERIALS

Bulky weight yarn

[100% acrylic, 3 ounces, 135 yards (85 grams, 338 meters) per skein]

    7 skeins white

Note: *Photographed model made with Lion Brand® Homespun® #309 Deco*

Size K (6.5 mm) crochet hook (or size required for gauge)

Yarn needle

GAUGE

12 sc = 5" (12.7 cm)

STITCH GUIDE

Ch: Chain

Sc: Single crochet

Dc: Double crochet

INSTRUCTIONS

Loosely ch 109.

Row 1: Sc in 2nd ch from hook and in each remaining ch: 108 sc; ch 1, turn.

Row 2: Sc in each sc; ch 1, turn.

Rows 3 through 5: Repeat Row 2.

Row 6: Sc in each sc, ch 3 (counts as first dc on following rows), turn.

Row 7: Dc in each sc, ch 1, turn.

Row 8: Sc in each dc, ch 3, turn.

Repeat Rows 7 and 8 until piece measures about 54" (137.16 cm) from begining ch, ending by working a Row 7.

Last Rows: Work 6 rows in sc.

Finish off and weave in ends.

Easy Scarf

Here's a wonderful pattern if you are just learning to crochet, or if you need a scarf in a hurry.

SKILL LEVEL

Beginner

FINISHED SIZE

Approx 8" x 72" (20.32 cm x 182.88 cm)

MATERIALS:

Worsted weight yarn

[100% acrylic, 5 ounces, 230 yards (141 grams, 211 meters) per skein]

    1 skein multi-color (A)

[100% acrylic, 7 ounces, 370 yards (198 grams, 338 meters) per skein]

    1 skein raspberry (B)

Note: *Photographed model made with Red Heart® With Love® #1942 Plum Jam (A) and #1701 Hot Pink (B)*

Size J (6 mm) crochet hook (or size required for gauge)

Yarn needle

GAUGE

16 dc = 4" (10.16 cm)

STITCH GUIDE

Ch: Chain

Dc: Double crochet

Sc: Single crochet

INSTRUCTIONS

Half of scarf (make 2)

With A, ch 26.

Row 1 (right side): Dc in 4th ch from hook (beginning 3 skipped chs count as first dc), dc in each remaining ch across: 24 dc; ch 3 (counts as first dc on following rows), turn.

Row 2: Dc in each st across, change to B, ch 1, turn.

Row 3: Sc in back loop of each stitch across, ch 1, turn.

Row 4: Sc in each sc across, ch 1, turn.

Row 5: Repeat Row 4.

Row 6: Sc in each stitch across, change to A, ch 3, turn.

Row 7: Dc in each stitch across, ch 3, turn.

Rows 8 through 97: Repeat Rows 2 through 7 fifteen times.

Rows 98 and 99: Repeat Rows 2 and 3.

Row 100: Sc in each stitch across. Finish off and weave in ends.

Finishing

With right sides together, sew across last row.

Traditional Granny Throw

Designed by Katherine Eng for Red Heart®

The traditional black-bordered, brightly colored granny square throw is always in fashion. It's easy to do and fun to make. Feel free to come up with your own unique color combination, or just follow our pattern.

SKILL LEVEL

Easy

FINISHED SIZE

Approx 50" x 58" (127 cm x 147.76 cm)

MATERIALS

Worsted weight yarn

[100% acrylic, 7 ounces, 370 yards (198 grams, 338 meters) per skein]

> 2 skeins black (A)

> 1 skein each orange (B), green (C), blue (D), purple (E), yellow (F) and dark red (G)

Note: *Photographed model made with Red Heart® With Love® #1012 Black, #1252 Mango, #1562 Jadeite, #1814 True Blue, #1538 Lilac, #1207 Cornsilk and #1914 Berry Red*

Size J (6 mm) crochet hook (or size required for gauge)

Size I (5.5 mm) crochet hook

Yarn needle

GAUGE

With J hook: Rounds 1 and 2 = 3½" (8.89 cm)

STITCH GUIDE

Ch: Chain

Sl st: Slip stitch

Dc: Double crochet

INSTRUCTIONS

Squares

Make 42 squares, 7 of each color combination.

COLOR COMBINATIONS

Square 1: E, C, D, G and B

Square 2: D, B, F, C and E

Square 3: F, E, D, B and C

Square 4: B, G, C, E and F

Square 5: C, D, E, B and G

Square 6: G, F, B, C and D

With first color and J hook, ch 4; join with sl st in first ch to form ring.

Round 1(right side): Ch 3 (counts as first dc here and on following rows), 2 dc in ring, ch 2, (3 dc in ring, ch 2) 3 times; join with sl st in 3rd ch of beginning ch-3: 12 dc, 4 ch-2 spaces. Finish off.

Round 2: With right side facing and J hook, join 2nd color in any ch-2 space, ch 3, (2 dc, ch 2, 3 dc) in same space, ch 1, * (3 dc, ch 2, 3 dc) in next ch-2 space, ch 1; repeat from * around; join with sl st in 3rd ch of turning ch-3: 24 dc, 4 ch-2 spaces and 4 ch-1 spaces. Finish off.

Round 3: With right side facing and J hook, join 3rd color in any ch-1 space, ch 3, 2 dc in same space, *ch 1, (3 dc, ch 2, 3 dc) in next ch-2 space, ch 1 **, 3 dc in next ch-1 space; repeat from * around, ending last

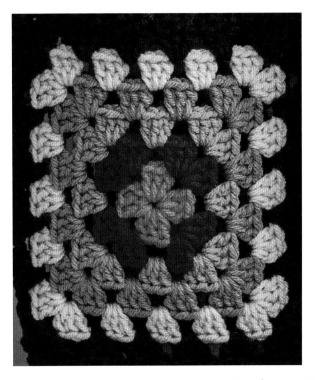

43

instructions continued on page 44

repeat at **; join with sl st in 3rd ch of turning ch-3: 36 dc, 4 ch-2 spaces and 8 ch-1 spaces. Finish off.

Round 4: With right side facing and J hook, join 4th color in first ch-1 space to left of any ch-2 space, ch 3, 2 dc in same space, *ch 1, 3 dc in next ch-1 space, ch 1, (3 dc, ch 2, 3 dc) in next ch-2 space, ch 1 **, 3 dc in next ch-1 space; repeat from * around, ending last repeat at **; join with sl st in 3rd ch of turning ch-3: 48 dc, 4 ch-2 spaces and 12 ch-1 spaces. Finish off.

Round 5: With right side facing and J hook, join 5th color in first ch-1 space to left of any ch-2 space, ch 3, 2 dc in same space, *ch 1, (3 dc in next ch-1 space, ch 1) twice, (3 dc, ch 2, 3 dc) in next ch-2 space, ch 1 **, 3 dc in next ch-1 space; repeat from * around, ending last repeat at **; join with sl st in 3rd ch of turning ch-3: 60 dc, 4 ch-2 spaces and 16 ch-1 spaces. Finish off.

Round 6: With right side facing and J hook, join A in first ch-1 space to left of any ch-2 space, ch 3, 2 dc in same space, *ch 1, (3 dc in next ch-1 space, ch 1) 3 times, (3 dc, ch 4, 3 dc) in next ch-2 space, ch 1 **, 3 dc in next ch-1 space; repeat from * around, ending last repeat at **; join with sl st in 3rd ch of turning ch-3: 72 dc, 4 ch-4 spaces and 20 ch-1 spaces. Finish off.

Assembly

With right sides facing, sew squares together through back loops following Diagram.

Border

Round 1: With right side facing and J hook, join A with sl st in any ch-1 space to left of any corner ch-4 space; ch 3, 2 dc in same space; * ch 1, (3 dc, ch 1) in each ch-1 space and in each joined ch-4 space across to next corner ch-4 space; (3 dc, ch 4, 3 dc) in corner ch-4 space; repeat from * 3 times more; ch 1; join with sl st in 3rd ch of beginning ch-3.

Round 2: With I hook, sl st in next dc, ch 1, (sc, ch 2, sc) in same dc, * ch 1, sl st in next ch-1 space, ch 1, (sc, ch 2, sc) in 2nd dc of next 3-dc group; repeat from * across to next corner ch-4 space; ch 1, (sc, ch 2, sc, ch 3, sc, ch 2, sc) in corner ch-4 space; ** ch 1, sl st in next ch-1 space, ch 1, (sc, ch 2, sc) in 2nd dc of next 3-dc group; repeat from ** across to next corner ch-4 space; ch 1, (sc, ch 2, sc, ch 3, sc, ch 2, sc) in corner ch-4 space; *** ch 1, sl st in next ch-1 space, ch 1, (sc, ch 2, sc) in 2nd dc of next 3-dc group; repeat from *** across to next corner ch-4 space; ch 1, (sc, ch 2, sc, ch 3, sc, ch 2, sc) in corner ch-4 space; **** ch 1, sl st in next ch-1 space, ch 1, (sc, ch 2, sc) in 2nd dc of next 3-dc group; repeat from **** across to next corner ch-4 space; ch 1, (sc, ch 2, sc, ch 3, sc, ch 2, sc) in corner ch-4 space; ch 1, sl st in next ch-1 space, ch 1; join with sl st in first sc.

Finish off and weave in ends.

1	2	3	4	5	6
6	5	4	3	2	1
1	2	3	4	5	6
6	5	4	3	2	1
1	2	3	4	5	6
6	5	4	3	2	1
1	2	3	4	5	6

Assembly Diagram

Stitches

Slipknot

Almost all crochet starts by first making a slipknot (or slip loop) on the hook

Step 1: Place yarn end on a flat surface, keeping a 6" end, and making a loop.

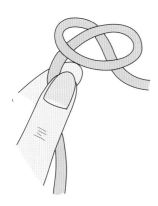

Step 2: Insert hook as shown and draw up a loop onto the hook by pulling on end marked A. Slipknot should slide easily on the hook.

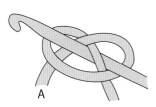

Make certain to leave loose yarn end about 6" long for weaving in later.

Chain Stitch

Step 1: Make slipknot on the hook.

Step 2: Bring yarn from back to front over hook and draw it through the loop on the hook. You have now made one chain stitch.

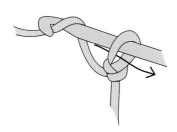

Step 3: Again bring the yarn from the back to the front over the hook and draw it through the loop on the hook. You have now made 2 chain stitches.

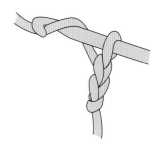

Continue to repeat step 3 until you have the desired number of chains.

Slip Stitch

Step 1: Insert hook in specified stitch, chain, or loop.

Step 2: Yarn over and draw hook through stitch, chain or loop, and loop on hook in one motion.

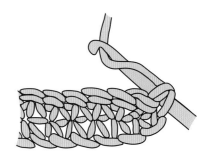

Single Crochet

Step 1: Insert hook in specified chain and draw up a loop: 2 loops on hook.

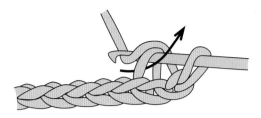

Step 2: Yarn over and draw the hook through both loops on the hook.

Single crochet completed.

Half Double Crochet

Step 1: Yarn over, insert hook into third chain from the hook, yarn over and draw up loop: 3 loops are now on the hook.

Step 2: Yarn over again and draw yarn through all 3 loops on the hook at one time: one half double crochet stitch is completed.

Repeat Steps 1 and 2 in each stitch across the row; however in Step 1, insert the hook in the next chain instead of third chain from the hook.

Double Crochet

Step 1: Yarn over from back to front; skip first 3 chains from hook, and insert hook in back bump of fourth chain.

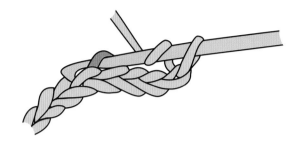

Step 2: Yarn over and draw through chain stitch and up onto working area of the hook: 3 loops remain on the hook.

Step 3: Yarn over and draw through the first two loops on the hook: 2 loops remain on the hook.

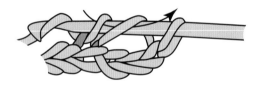

Step 4: Yarn over again and draw through both loops on the hook. One double crochet stitch completed.

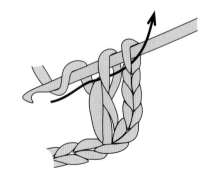

Special Helps

Joining Yarn

When joining a new ball of yarn, try to make it at the end of a row whenever possible. Make certain that you will have enough yarn to complete a row before you start it. Work the last stitch in the row until one final step remains. Then drop the old yarn to the back, leaving the loop on the hook. Cut the old yarn off, leaving a 6" yarn end for weaving in later. Hold the new yarn behind the work and complete the last step of the stitch with the new yarn.

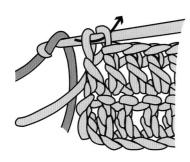

Make the turning chain with the new yarn and continue with it. If you need to change colors in the middle of a row, use the same technique, working the last step of the final stitch in the old color with the new color. Cut the old color and continue with the new color.

Finishing Off

When you have finished a crochet piece, cut the yarn several inches beyond the last stitch worked, leaving a 6" end. Draw the end through the last loop remaining on the hook. This will prevent the work from unraveling.

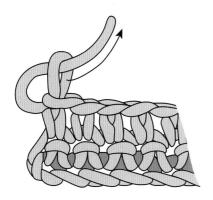

Weaving in the Ends

When you have completed all of your crocheting, you may find yarn ends just hanging there loosely. Thread the ends in a yarn needle. Working on the wrong side of your crocheting, weave the needle in and out of the backs of several of your stitches. Then weave again in another direction. Weave about 2" in one direction and 1" in the opposite direction. Trim off any extra yarn.

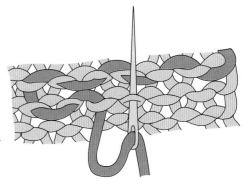

Never permit your yarn needle to go through to the front of the project.

Standard Yarn Weights

To make it easier for yarn manufacturers, publishers, and designers to prepare consumer-friendly products and for consumers to select the right materials for a project, the following standard yarn weight system has been adopted.

Standard Yarn Weight System
Categories of yarn, gauge, ranges, and recommended needle and hook sizes

Yarn Weight Symbol & Category	0 Lace	1 Super Fine	2 Fine	3 Light	4 Medium	5 Bulky	6 Super Bulky	7 Jumbo
Type of Yarns in Category	Fingering 10 count crochet thread	Sock Fingering, Baby	Sport, Baby	DK, Light, Worsted	Worsted, Afghan, Aran	Chunky, Craft, Rug	Super Bulky, Roving	Jumbo, Roving
Crochet Gauge* Ranges in Single Crochet to 4 inch	32-42 double crochets**	21-32 sts	16-20 sts	12-17 sts	11-14 sts	8-11 sts	6-9 sts	5 sts and fewer
Recommended Hook in Metric Size Range	Steel*** 1.6-1.4mm	2.25-3.5mm	3.5-4.5mm	4.5-5.5mm	5.5-6.5mm	6.5-9mm	9-16mm	16mm and larger
Recommended Hook US Size Range	Steel*** 6, 7, 8 Regular hook B-1	B-1 to E-4	E-4 to 7	7 to I-9	I-9 to K-10 1/2	K-10 1/2 to M-13	M-13 to Q	Q and larger

*GUIDELINES ONLY: The above reflect the most commonly used gauges and needle or hook sizes for specific yarn categories.

**Lace weight yarns are usually crocheted on larger hooks to create lacy, openwork patterns. Accordingly, a gauge range is difficult to determine. Always follow the gauge stated in your pattern.

*** Steel crochet hooks are sized differently from regular hooks—the higher the number, the smaller the hook, which is the reverse of regular hook sizing.

Skill Levels

Yarn manufacturers, publishers, needle and hook manufacturers have worked together to set up a series of guidelines and symbols to bring uniformity to patterns. Before beginning a project, check to see if your skill level is equal to the one listed for the project.

Beginner — Projects for first-time crocheters using basic stitches and minimal shaping.

Easy — Projects using yarn with basic stitches, repetitive stitch patterns, simple color changes, and simple shaping and finishing.

Intermediate — Projects using a variety of techniques, such as basic lace patterns or color patterns, mid-level shaping and finishing.

Experienced — Projects with intricate stitch patterns, techniques and dimension, such as non-repeating patterns, multi-color techniques, fine threads, small hooks, detailed shaping and refined finishing.